GETTING THROUGH IT

BY MARK GOULD

CHAPTERS:

content warning

This book contains literary descriptions of disturbing subjects that may not be appropriate for certain readers, below are listed <u>some</u> of the disturbing subjects you will encounter.

Overdosis, self harm, suicide, drug abuse, suicide attempts, murder, school shootings, general violence, descriptive depictions of death.

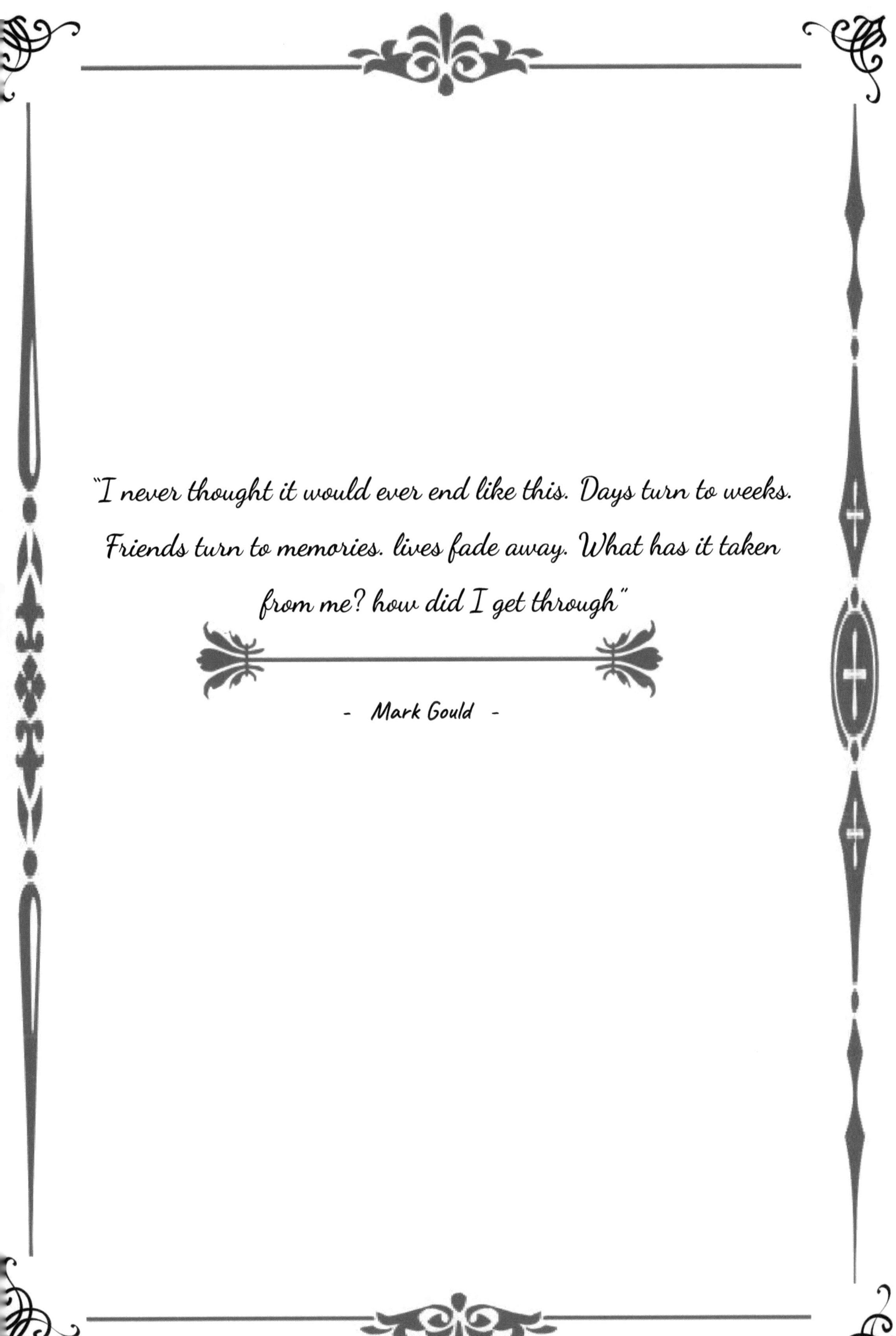

"I never thought it would ever end like this. Days turn to weeks. Friends turn to memories. lives fade away. What has it taken from me? how did I get through"

- Mark Gould -

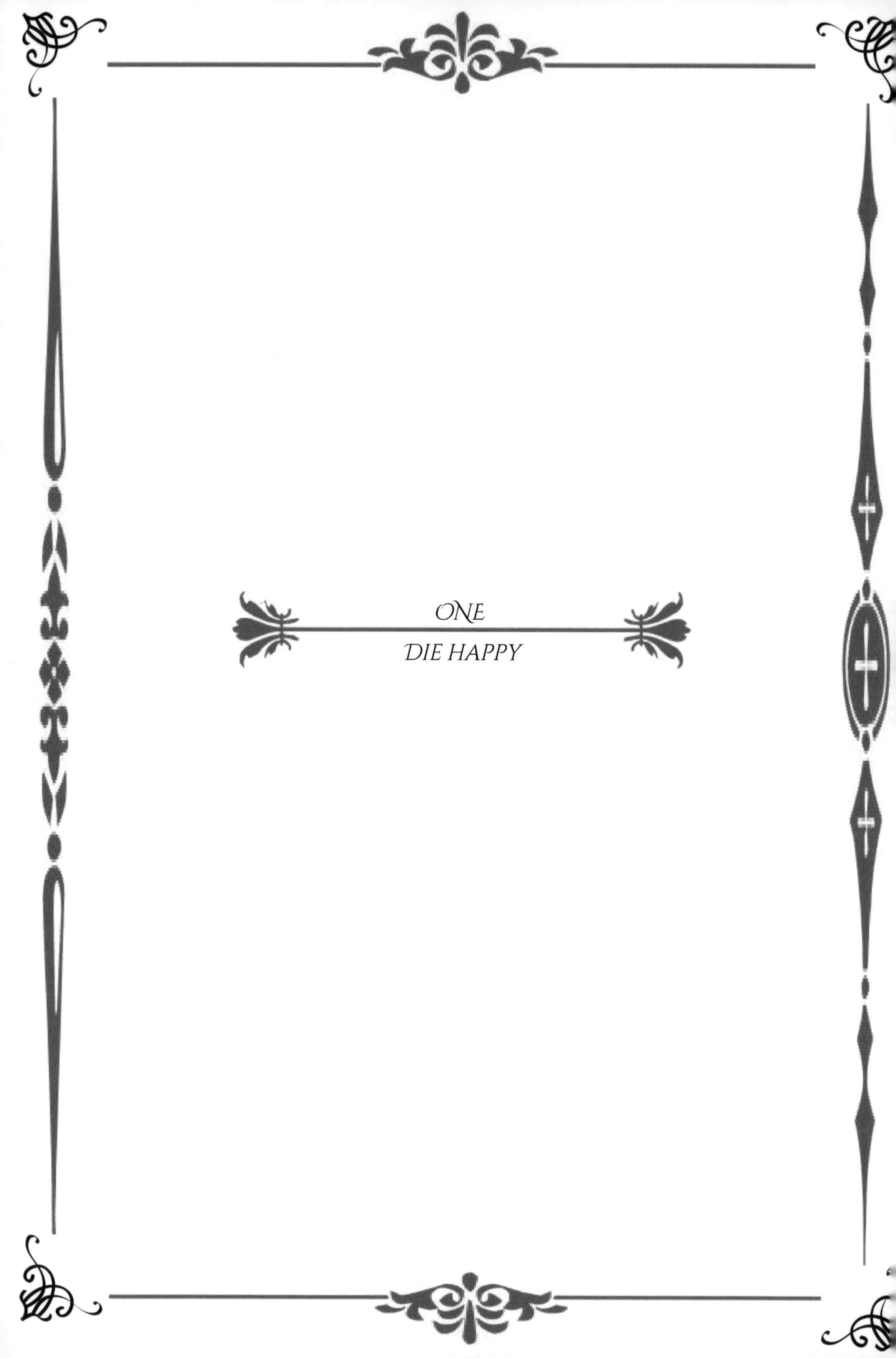

ONE
DIE HAPPY

Lingering

you feel it, in your stomach, that's where it lingers. It is there every day. Sometimes it's strong, other times it's controllable.

When you accept that this is how you feel, it starts to eat at you from the inside. You get a lack of feeling and a lack of caring about yourself and everything else.
Your brain goes into self-defense mode as it shuts down. It makes everything pointless, and you wander around in a body you don't recognize anymore.

What can I do when I don't feel anything? It's an empty feeling.
It lingers in your soul and makes you paralyzed to the world around you. You are a prisoner of your own mind. You feel only sadness and hopelessness. You don't want to do anything other than feel the pain and suffering. You know that is the only thing you can do, so you bite the bullet every day. And as it lingers in you, you linger in the body. Not caring about anything.

It's a weird comfort to go into the darkness, to give in to the emotion. At what point should I give in to mine? Last time I did, I tried to kill myself. I would say I hope I don't find out when the next time is, but the truth is, I don't care about it. All I see death as is mercy, sparing a soul of torture.

Hope hurts

Hope. Hope is a feeling that hurts.

Every time you feel hope is there, you realize you have to live with the things you have done. How do you get back to a normal life when these scars are so permanent? Sure, happiness might come back at some point, but what about holding a knife without thinking about that one time? How will I be able to take pills without the thought of taking more? How can I live a life if I have been scarred too much from a part of my childhood?

Hope is scary to me.

Hopelessness means giving up and giving in. It means being lost.

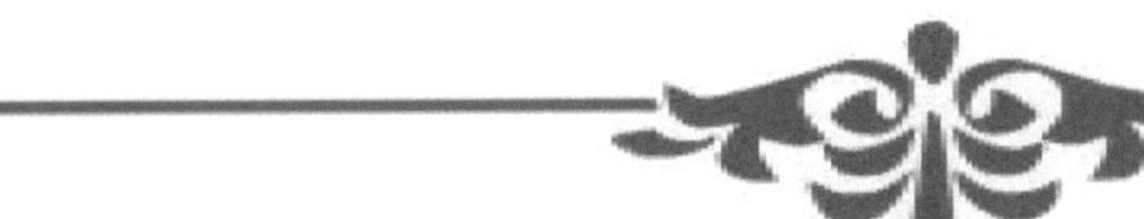

Hope means seeing a path that you can take, but the path is scary and dangerous. You know you will tumble, you will bruise yourself. Sometimes, I think it's easier to linger in hopelessness. Guess it's easier to live without the regrets of the past.

Rain

I like the rain. The rain is in harmony with my feelings. When it rains, you often feel limited and isolated. The rain invites you to reflect, to take it slow, and to enjoy simple comforts. For me, the rain captures the feeling of being a prisoner of a lack of feeling.

The rain is something I can look at. I can get lost in the small drops. The weirdly calming sensation rain can have on me is like no other. Listening to a sad and peaceful song while the rain pours fills me with acceptance.

I feel betrayed and beaten by the universe. I am still waiting for the scale to stabilize. The rain speaks to me and asks me to slow down, to accept that this is how I feel, and that nothing but time can truly heal me.

Rain is a form of hope. Rain is trying to start the next chapter of one's story. The rain says it's okay to hurt, it's okay to hurt.

Routines of pain

When breaking becomes the habit,
 When darkness is there, you look at it.
 When routines of pain become mundane to explain.

When you start to adjust,
 Only to break that trust.

How can one find a life worth living in a routine of pain? How can one find meaning when you feel this way? When you start to settle into the darkness—settle into the darkness and despair, the utter lack of hoping for a way out.

What do you do when you're not strong enough to keep fighting and too weak to end it?

You're stuck in your emotions, stuck in the torture of being, scared to ask for death.

I don't know how to live with any of this, yet this pain becomes a routine. In routines of pain, of time in a place you don't want to be. I keep dragging myself down every time, going back to the routine. Guess I am too scared to truly try and leave it all behind.

So I stay in the spiral of pain. It's killing me and taking too much, yet it keeps eating me over and over—a routine of taking parts of me. That routine can't go on forever.

Emotional insanity

When do you lose your mind to insanity?

The definition of insanity is when the mind takes over and a person becomes unreasonable and unsound.

I just feel empty or filled with sadness and anger. It's hurting my mental state, making everything unbearable. Bearing this pain on my body for so long, it starts to crack. When I crack, I am unreasonable. I lash out at people. I become a broken human, filled with emotions too strong to keep inside—randomly crying, suddenly wanting to punch the walls.

The body needs to let go of the emotion, and it doesn't know how. It can't let go of the amount of emotion—tears, screaming, hurting yourself. None of it works. None of it is enough to express the pain I am in. The one thing that expresses how I feel is when I take a lethal overdose of pills. Guess then I am expressing the pain I am in.

If someone cries in front of you, it's to let you know they are sad and not okay. And when they tell you they just took too many pills, they are saying they can't keep living like this. Suicide is a form of expression.

The only time I felt truly happy in over a year was when I expressed my feelings—when I took too many pills. Because I finally got all my emotions out. I got it all out because killing myself is the only way I could ever express how this feels.

Humans are designed to break, yet I break every day, every minute. I can't escape the cycle of violent emotions ripping my mental load apart. I am at full capacity, but life keeps filling me up with more and more.

The river has a season where it fills up with streams running from the mountains or from a heavy rain season. There is balance in the dry seasons and the rainy seasons. But the rain kept pouring, and the water overstayed its welcome. The river overflows into a waterfall, spilling over the edge, taking the driftwood and weak plants around it downstream and over the cliff. The constant pressure of gravity greets the pull and drags everything down.

In the same way, my brain drags me down. As I fight against the current, the driftwood turns into tree trunks that hurl downstream, crashing into me. The closer I come to the edge, the harder the journey back up again. But if you find a branch to hold onto near the edge, you would rather hold onto the branch than try your luck at swimming against the waterfall. You can't beat gravity.

My brain is like a dried river.

My mind keeps dragging me down and making me unstable. I am so unstable I can't trust myself anymore—not my feelings, not my actions, not my core beliefs.

I doubt everything around me. I am losing my mind and would rather let go of the branch than see where I end up if I keep holding on.

I am losing my mind. I must be going insane, bit by bit.

Peace of mind

Peace,
 Peace of mind.

The only time I feel peace of mind is when I give myself the drugs to avoid the thoughts. Upon taking a deadly overdose of pills, I got peace of mind because I thought I had finally made my choice. There was peace in letting it all go, in finally seeing an end to it all. There is no point in asking any more questions. There is no point in asking yourself if taking those pills was a bad idea.

What's done is done and cannot be undone.

The peace I got when I laid down by my friends, who were worried about me. I am surrounded by those that love me. A better end I couldn't ask for, but death had other plans.

They say you will regret the attempt if you survive it. I don't regret it. I am only mad because I failed. Why would I be sad if it gave me a feeling of happiness? I would, with pleasure, trade my life for 1–2 hours of happiness before I drift off into death.

I would take it in a heartbeat to not feel my heartbeat.

The peace I get from letting go is heavenly. I still want to die. I am still angry and disappointed when I wake up.

The day that shouldn't be

18 June 2024

18 June 2024 is the day after my attempt.

Waking up, I felt a strange, new feeling. I felt sad, filled with despair. I wasn't supposed to see the light of day. Yesterday, I was supposed to have died. The world was supposed to keep turning, and I felt so uncomfortable about still breathing. The only thing I could think about was finishing the job.

I wasn't supposed to be here. I wasn't supposed to see this, hear what I heard, listen to the birds, wake up to the alarm, look out the window, look my friends in the eyes, or look at myself in the mirror and see a person who doesn't want to exist. I wasn't supposed to be conscious of what happened and still be here. I wasn't supposed to be here... but I am.

I am still suffering. I didn't break the routine. To rise above this, I had to face the fact that I tried to end my life twice. I had no energy left in my body, so I just laid in bed, wasting away. All I wanted and still want is to waste away. I don't want to get better in a world that no longer feels like mine. I don't feel at home here. Every day since has felt off. Everything has gotten worse, and I still don't feel like I belong here, or anywhere.

That day, I wasted away, punishing myself for failing. I was so ready to die. I had given my pills to others to keep me safe after I told them about my overdose. Now, I was a soul that just wanted to die. I felt like my only purpose was to die, and I had taken that ability away. Somehow, I am feeling sadness beyond suicide.

I still regret not taking more pills that day. I still feel like my mind has made peace with the choice of suicide. Now, it feels as if my mind has already decided my fate. How can I fight myself when I've already made the decision?

Time feels like it's at a standstill. Time doesn't matter when you don't feel like you belong here.

Sleep, food, friendships, interests, hobbies, work, money—none of it feels relevant when all you want is to die.

I try so hard to give my life meaning through writing, trying to express with words what others may not be able to, trying to give myself purpose beyond myself, trying to help others who may be in a similar place. It's wishful thinking that I'm helping anyone with my writing, but I still try. I try so my mind can find a reason to stay. And so, I live through another day in a place where I don't belong.

Die happy

17 June 2024

I stand with them in my hands. "It's only 5.5 pills," I say to myself, knowing deaths have been seen at lower doses.

I take them one by one, crying with each swallow, knowing this might be my end. My pills have amphetamine in them, and it can cause heart attacks if enough is digested. Drinking from the gray metal bottle, it makes a hollow loud sound as I put it softly down on the table. The mind is sad but filled with adrenaline.

I lived in a dormitory and called on some friends to come over. One of them comes through the door. I look into her eyes as tears start to roll out. Her worried look meets mine as I try to form a sentence.

"I…I took a lethal dose this time," I say.
 "I think it's best you take this from me." She took the pills, but little did she know, I had a friend I cheated into giving me 5 more pills, and I took them all a little later, knowing that 10.5 pills would do the trick. I was surrounded by friends, all worried for my health; I wasn't.

They felt my heart, my heartbeat, as it faded in and out of consciousness. As I closed my eyes, I could feel myself drifting. I could feel my mind accepting that I am going to be gone. I felt harmony in leaving. I let go of all my worries and went to sleep.

Waking up to a faint voice being my friends, the longer I took to respond, the louder they got. Other times, I would jolt awake with big muscle spasms. The bloodstreams were beginning to fill up. After laying in a bed, drifting and being kept awake by friends, I got mad over the fact that it didn't happen yet, it didn't work yet. I started crying uncontrollably, bursting out in a high voice, screaming and sobbing, "It was supposed to work! THIS! WAS SUPPOSED TO WORK!"

My body felt defeated and went back to sobbing for about 1 hour. After that, I laid down and made the time go by. At one point, I heard voices. I am not kidding here, it can be a side effect of an overdose of the medicine I had in my blood. I heard my friends say, "Hey Mark." I answered by saying, "What?" but no one had said anything.

Once, I heard the sound of one of them when I was alone. All of a sudden, I couldn't feel my heartbeat. My friends started to panic because they couldn't feel it either. I felt fear and excitement. I looked at my friends as they desperately tried to find it, saying I still have a pulse. At the same time, I saw how they weren't ready to let me go. Not a lot of people have those kinds of friends, and I was lucky to have them.

They found my heartbeat around 3 minutes later. I looked into her eyes and, in an afraid and low tone, said, "I can't feel it, emmm, I can't feel it, I can't feel my heartbeat." She tried to calm me as I felt my veins start to harden up. But time passed, and I realized that somehow, 10.5 pills wasn't enough. I didn't get much sleep when they followed me to my room as I laid in bed.

What's gonna happen now? What am I going to face when I open my eyes tomorrow? What will be staring back at me?

There are things in life you can move on from. Maybe it's a crush you didn't ask for, or maybe it's a dumb argument that leads to some loose consequences.

Then, there are things you can't let go, things that don't heal over time. It's the tragedies and traumas that shape us into humans. Letting go of a loved one. Saying goodbye. Realizing your own deep flaws. It's things that shake you to the core. These moments are meant to be good, like a first kiss, but the last moments of my childhood were spent alone, crying. And my start as an adult was spent facing the fact that, as an 18-year-old, I tried to kill myself.

Many of my scars are permanent, like those memories. I can't learn to live a life where I can get over trying to end it, and I am scared to take the next step forward with these scars on my mind. I have to live with the fact that I don't want to. It's scary to know that, after you choose, whether it's an attempt or a success, there are always consequences. I am shaped anew from these scars.

The river is empty and dried up, with logs and stones filling up the river, leaving it forever dried up. Marks from the waterfall are everywhere.

It will never be the same.

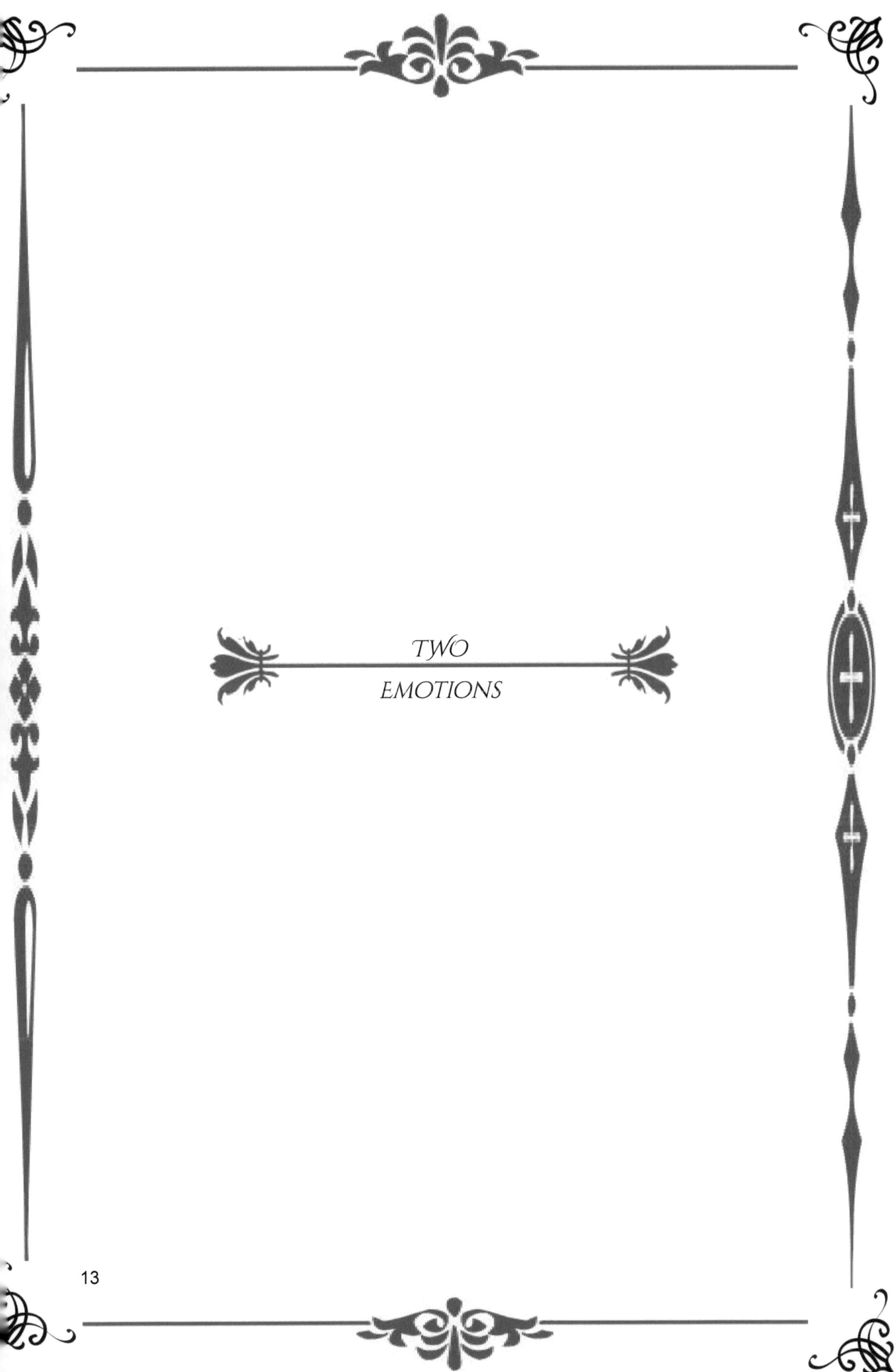

TWO
EMOTIONS

Bleeding internally

Emotion is silent. It spreads like a virus. It slowly takes over every part of you. It starts off small; you can't explain it to friends and family, but you are just a little distant. You don't have as much energy, and you start to make excuses. But you feel it deep down, brewing and boiling you from the inside.

Each day, it lingers in the background, adding to your mental capacity day by day. Once you realize that something is off, it's often too late. It was for me.

You try to get through the week, but the routine you have made gets hard to keep. You need to be with yourself. You start to blame yourself for feeling this way. You start to hate yourself for being this way. You start to cry more, feel more, you break more.

While everyone around you moves forward, you move back deeper and deeper into your own hell, in the center of your mind and thoughts. While everyone around you goes through life, you go through hell without them noticing or truly caring. No one can understand your pain. You have thought of everything, and the thoughts regularly overwhelm you, dragging you down a spiral of despair. There is nothing anyone can tell or do for you to make you feel better. They can't make heaven out of hell.

You are helplessly hanging on to the sinking ship that is your mental state. You are drowning slowly, surrounded in water with cement shoes. When your emotions overwhelm you, they are your worst enemy. The only way to defeat such an enemy is to kill it.

When your worst enemy is yourself, how do you win?

The storm

How does it feel?

How can someone describe the hurricane in my mind? The storm of emotion switching between anger, sadness, and frustration.

Imagine you're on a small fishing boat. You are the captain. There's a storm raging.

You are too far out for anyone to come to your aid, nothing but miles upon miles of ocean. The water is freezing. The night sky is filled with stars. The air is ice cold, and the wind is like small needles piercing through any exposed skin. The small fishing boat was not built for such weather. It's way out of its depth. The waves are like skyscrapers, rising up to the heavens. Every wave crashes into the boat, shaking it, tossing it around like leaves in the wind. You try to get control of the boat, but it's no use. You're panicking. You look around. Waves are coming in from every side, surrounding you, as your screams are drowned out by the waves crashing against the hull of the boat. You get tossed around, trying to keep your balance. You barely have time to assess the situation before another wave hits, throwing you to the hard metal hull once again. You are out alone on the sea. No one is coming to save you. No one knows you're here. They're all laying in bed, comfortable, sleeping while you suffer. Mother nature is cruel. The chaotic nature of your situation makes it hard to think straight. The ocean is unforgiving and takes no prisoners. The boat nearly tips over because of the waves. At what point do you stop trying to fight the storm and get control of the ship? At what point do you give in and look for a life vest?

Everyone else in the world doesn't know your struggle.

They don't know the extent of your fight.

While they sleep, I lay awake crying. While they laugh, I am fighting. While they live, I am dying.

So, if you want to know what this feels like, try being neglected. Try being alone. Try being abandoned. From where I am standing, I am left to fend for myself, but we all know that a captain is nothing without his crew.

Worthy

Being alone can be hard, feeling betrayed can be even harder, but to not feel worthy, that's a knife to the heart.

Being alone is not a problem, but it's the feeling of being lonely that's hard.

Many times I cry alone. The ones I love use their time with others, leaving me feeling worthless. No matter who you have by your side, this battle is one you and you alone can fight. Yet having someone to be there shows support. Why won't they be there when you need them? Have you not deserved their aid, their help, their love, and care? Are you not worthy of such things? Not to them? What even are you to them? Something less than human?

Humans can be so cold. I just need their love. Is that too much to ask for after everything we have been through, calling each other friends? All that time is a waste if it doesn't mean anything to them—at least it doesn't mean enough for them to help you. And the worst part is, you start to believe you are not worthy of their help, when the truth is, they are not deserving of your friendship and endless kindness. You don't want to lose them, and you may do so if you use them. If you speak your mind about their lack of support, they will leave you behind.

As a human, I would rather kill myself than be lonely. I would rather drown myself in pills than ask them to hold me. I don't want to lose them, but it seems I never had them in the first place.

I started to do self-harm. I would use a necklace or a steak knife. I would listen to music—sad music—and I would start to scream internally. Each stroke of the knife was another thing I couldn't get myself to say to them:

Why aren't you here for me? What have I done to deserve this? Do you even care if I am okay?

Why are you just walking away from me? Why are you giving others what I want?

The blade is dull, so I cut faster and faster, again and again, simultaneously crying with each stroke, getting angrier as I start to weep. Tears mix with blood and snot. Bloodshot eyes get desperate.

Is this love? Is this friendship? Why are you treating me like this? Do you even know how much your support would mean to me? Why am I not worthy? Why am I not worthy?

Emotion

Around 14 June 2024

It's late. I ask for a friend over messenger, a simple ask:
"Help me, I don't know how, but help me."
Less than a minute later, she was with me. Anger fills me up, anger for the fact that life has decided to make itself difficult.
At this point, it's really fucking difficult. I ask for them to hold me, and I feel my body become heavy. My head collides with the wall, half resting on the cold iron lamp. I close my eyes, squeezing my eyelashes together as hard as I can, letting out a painful whimpering sob as tears flow through. As the tears appear between my eyes again, anger fills me, and I start to scream. The friend tries to calm me, but I don't want to be calm anymore.
"I can't do this anymore," I say, stumbling as the tears choke my ability to speak.
By now, my shirt and pillow are soaked. Anger, anger is what is left. It always shows its ugly and disturbing face when you're around those that you least want it to go out on. The emotions grow and grow to a size my body cannot handle. I break down and can do nothing but cry. At that moment, I realized I could not hold myself back anymore.
I realized that I hated everything around me. At that moment, I chose to defeat myself. I surrendered to the feelings one last time. When you can't express how you feel and you're not dead yet, you just cry, and so I did, don't know for how long. Every thought of true peace came forth as I knew I was going to try to end it any day now.
The tears were because I realized that my life won't have a happy ending. That I wanted to die so fucking bad that I was going to do it. I was scared of myself. I was my own murderer, and you can't run from yourself. This moment was me giving in. No longer did I have the mindset of trying to stay alive. I had the mindset of when I wanted to end it, and how. Tears rolled evermore, I shook, and curled up into a ball. I am a proper mess of a broken mind, one that has gone insane over the amount of emotions it has.
Emotion is a gift, but it can be poisonous if taken in large doses.
Being afraid of myself, not knowing what to do. Knowing there's nothing that can be done.
So I give up, I welcome the murderer into my home. I go outside the ship, leaving the lifevest in the helm.

So I ask, at what point is it dangerous to give into your emotions?
 At what point is the pain enough to warrant suicide?

The captain, alone, afraid, looks at a wave. It's big. The wave of emotion of the captain mirrors the wave he sees in front of him. It consumes the tiny fishing boat. The captain sinks into the dark unknown. The last thoughts of the captain were:
 "I know what I must do to end this madness, but I don't know if I am strong enough to do it."

THREE
DEMONS

Hurts

The pain. It won't stop. I can't make it stop.

Sometimes I wonder how hell could be worse than the so-called life I have. The pain is just mental, but it feels like physical pain. It's a drill drilling into the side of your skull. It's a needle piercing your pupils. The stomach feels like you have eaten a rose, each branch with thorns ripping you apart limb from limb. It feels like 40-pound weights are on your lungs. Your blood feels like it's cold, too cold. Your head feels like it's hitting the pavement from a 7-story building, and your heart feels like it's running a marathon. Your back feels like it's being pushed up against a bowling ball. Your feet feel immobilized.

How is this supposed to be living? Why is it me that has to feel this way? This pain is torture, like not being able to sleep, making the minutes stretch into hours. Try to live like I have, and you would realize that every second is an achievement. If this world knew mercy, I would have died that day. But I am still here, breathing, eating, walking, rotting, crying, cutting, dying. Alas, the world doesn't care about me. I just sit in a room expected to still function as a human when I am dying every second.

My cross

If there is evil, there shall always be light.
 Shadows only exist because of light. To keep away the demons, I use my Bible. My Bible is made of blood and sacrifice. My cross is sharp and poisonous. Every time I use it, I cut myself, and a bit of poison drips into my veins, finding its way to my heart.
 I call Abone, lesser evil, to fight my evil.
 Call a friend so you don't feel alone. You're not afraid of being alone; you're afraid of the thoughts that haunt you when you're alone. Like ghosts from your past, they reveal themselves as a new issue your brain has to manage.
 The friends can only take so much before they've heard it, before it becomes mundane.

But it's not your fault you feel this way all the time. Yet, you get punished by it anyway. You can't blame them for it, so do you blame yourself or nothing?

My cross takes parts of my soul. Each time I use it, I fall ever so deeper into self-hatred.
My cross is self-destructive. It's like basing a hammer against a wall, slowly deteriorating that wall. And once that wall is gone, what happens?
Once the wall comes down and the Bible is burned, the demons may feast. The circle is not sustainable.
Self-punishment is not sustainable. I am not sustainable.

My accessory

Accessories are a statement, one of who you want people to see you as.
Earrings may be cute or edgy. A necklace may depict you as a follower of a faith or club. Tattoos are a statement of something or someone you believe in, trust in. A tattoo is a statement. Cutting yourself is a statement. Cutting yourself is a statement of being low. It's a desperate cry for help that went unanswered. It's mental pain manifested into physical trauma. It's an expression of one's feelings. Maybe it's not meant for others to see, or maybe it is. But it's a sign from your brain to yourself. It's a sign saying to yourself that you can't handle this pain on your own. It's a sign of you finding comfort in the darkness, in taking the next step down the spiraling staircase that leads straight to hell.
Self-harm is acknowledging that the darkness has become a core part of your identity, and so you choose to show it, to wear it. You welcome the pain home and let it manifest in your body, taking over everything and turning you against yourself. Your eyes start to wander, bouncing around, looking for the thing that may quell some of the pain. Windows become jumping points. Mirrors become smashable painkillers. Knives become your next hit of adrenaline. Pills become your ability to sleep in a sleepless existence.

Demons

It's too much. I can feel it. This time, it's gonna win. This time, I'm gonna lose control of myself again.

Music plays loudly, and my brain realizes that the necklace I have on has a sharp edge. It's half a heart. It will be painful, and it will hurt. It's not a knife; it won't do the job smoothly.

It starts off slow. The sharp end of the necklace softly grazes the skin of my right leg. It runs over the same place it did last time. The thoughts come back. I know I will regret this, but I can't stop myself. In time with the music, I dig the end of the necklace into my skin, pressing it in, letting my muscle and flesh swallow half the damn thing. I lean it to one end so the corner of the tip digs a little deeper. It's uncomfortable, it hurts, and it's sickening that I am inflicting this on myself. I press it down and force it along my leg. It's not instant. It's getting caught between the hair on my leg. Not even blood yet.

I go again, sinking it deeper, going faster. I sink it down deep. Running it over the same place as I sit for a moment, contemplating, preparing myself to stroke down. I take a deep breath in.

I slowly move it forward. A stream of blood comes out behind it. As I run it down my leg, I whimper in pain and self-pity. Three lines of blood are there. I press my flesh around the wounds to make the blood appear. I look at the necklace, and the tip has amassed a collection of skin mixed with blood.

The emotion comes back, blinding me to the facts. Adrenaline kicks in as the music gets angry. I frantically cut with the heart up and down over the wound, making new wounds. It's like jumping horizontally across asphalt, scraping your leg against rough asphalt. Again and again. Tears run down as blood starts to run along every part of the leg. The wounds are deeper and go longer down. It all goes into one big mess of blood, half-erupted skin, and bloody hair remaining. The whipping is my brain seeing the consequence of its defeat, pleading for me to stop. The tears mix with the blood like rain connecting to other droplets to power their own trajectory. As I squeeze, a little bit of meat is seen. The salt from the tears mixes in like alcohol on an open wound. Each time a cut appears, it's another thing I blame myself for. Another reason to just end it.

Am I not enough? Cut.

I am not strong enough. Cut.

Where are my friends? Cut.

What have I even achieved in my life? Cut.

Will I ever be the same? Cut.

Where did my innocence go? Cut.

What is happening to me? Cut.

Am I to blame for these scars, or is it the diagnosis? Cut.

Why am I alone? Cut.

Am I not worthy of help? Cut.

I am so cold, so fucking cold. Where is my cross? Cut.

Why do I go through this hell every day? Cut.

And on it goes.

The necklace, once silver, now drips blood and has a metallic red look. What once was a statement of love is now a symbol of pain.

My hands have dried blood on them. My leg is dripping as my one sock has stains of blood on it. The bed I sleep in looks like a forensics table after a lobotomy. The accessory of that necklace now bears a new meaning. It stings in my leg as it's cramping up. My eyes are dry from crying, and my tone is nonexistent. I am left with my own mistakes. I am left contemplating and enduring the pulsing pain and lack of adrenaline as the silence of regret sets in.

You crawl ever deeper down the spiral. I wonder if it would be faster to just hurl yourself down the stairs. No, you don't need to. The bottom isn't far from here; you can feel it.

The demons will help you on your feet so you can get there. The darkness will help you. Isn't that a bit of comfort? You think to yourself. At least the darkness isn't abandoning me.

The necklace lurks in your line of sight, calling your name.

Maybe I should try the neck instead of the leg...

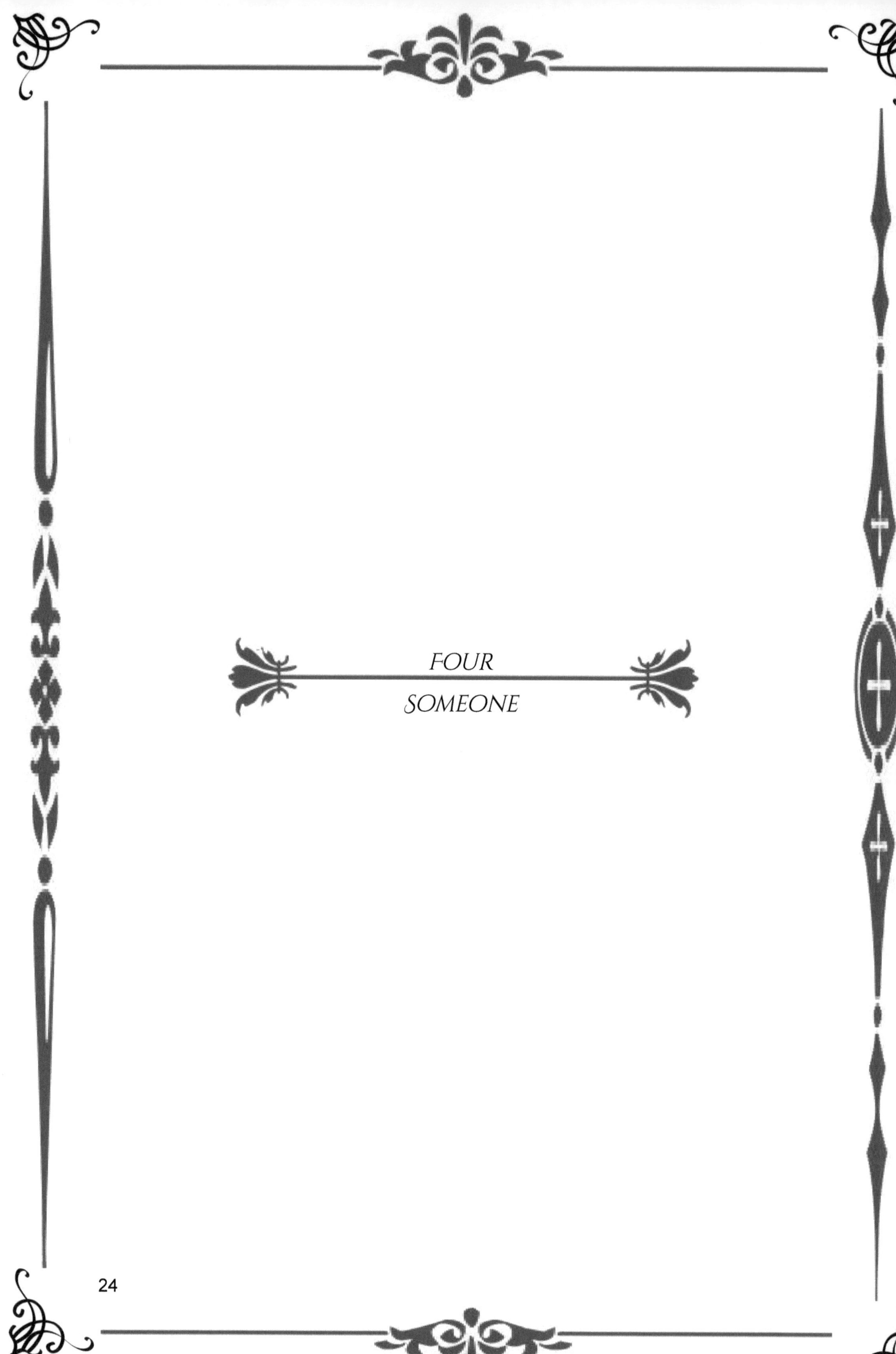

FOUR
SOMEONE

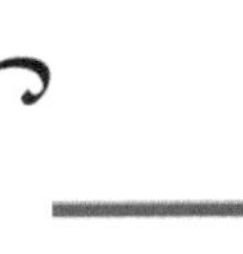

Letting someone in

Love.

Love is the best four-letter description of pain we have. I chose the drug that is love once. I let someone into my life fully. I gave more than I got. I sacrificed a part of myself for the hope that love would heal me, that they would heal me. I was wrong. In the end, I wasn't worthy in their eyes.

When you open up your heart to someone, you expect them to do the same. All I wanted was something normal, something real, but alas, the world found a way to twist the knife. Those who choose to be by my side through thick and thin are worthy, but she didn't. She had her reasons, and I had mine, but I expected something more than avoidance from her. I gave her my heart, but she seems hesitant to give me hers. I simply can't get mad at her; I am not built that way. So, I am left in a relationship where the partner avoids me when I am sad.

And I am always sad.

I let her in, and she was cold. She left me with nothing but questions she didn't want to answer. I gave in to her demands for space when I tried to kill myself. I might not have tried if I got the answers. I would rather kill myself than discomfort her. She is the last bit of light and happiness in my life, so I will do whatever I can to be worthy in her eyes, to get the key to her heart. She gave me the fake key, and I am the one who is locked.

Fake

Friends can be real, others can be fake.

Life will teach you to simply let someone go because they are not worth the struggle. This one goes out to a certain person in my life.

I gave you everything you wanted. I was there when you needed me, and you were my friend. Yet, you used me for your own selfish gain. For this, I cannot forgive you, and for what you have done to me, I cannot forget you.

You might be low, but I am lower. I only wanted to keep you around as a friend. I didn't deserve to be avoided by you. Can you truly give me a reason that isn't fake? At one time, we were friends, and I desperately wanted to keep it that way. But you pushed me away at every opportunity. I gave everything—my money, my time, and myself. What did I get in

return? You one day just fucking decided that I am no fun, that I was no longer useful to you. Like wrapping paper around a present, I was used and quickly thrown away. Not even a word on why. With proper communication and words, I could have forgiven you. But you abandoned this boat, and I was left on it alone, sinking. You were a bad friend, and you don't deserve the treatment you get from me or the world.

With a lot of people, I have sadness, anger, or disappointment to give. But with you, I only have three questions:

Why?

 Was it worth it?

 How do you feel?

I needed someone like you to anchor me to reality, but you did nothing. And now, I have tried to forgive you. I have tried to forget you. I know you're having a bad time, but I have tried to kill myself. Would you feel guilty if one of those calls you missed was my last attempt at staying?

 Would you have felt ashamed when you heard the church bells? Would you visit my grave, or would you not care? Would your heartless avoidance still shine? If I asked you, would you tell me the fucking truth or lie to me?

You wear a fake persona, and I don't know if I ever knew you. I don't know if you want to know this new you. If I succeeded in killing myself on June 17, 2024, would you have felt bad?

 Would you even have felt at all?

What I have given

I did everything in my power to make you comfortable. I used money, poetry, gifts, and so much more. I would get a "thanks," but nothing more.

 I would lie and not show my true emotional state, giving you the blissful unawareness of my pain. I held myself together only for you. You took so much of my mental capacity.

 I held back my anger and complaints about the utter lack of compassion and attraction you showed towards me. I held it all back, hoping it was because this would last a lot longer than it did. In holding it all back, I started to hurt myself. The music was about the lack of

everything in you, the bleeding was your doing. You made my emotional scars so deep they became physical.

You left me without closure or dignity. You kept attacking me. Did you think you were the victim in this? Tell me, what have you truly given? I have taken pills trying to end myself, and I didn't tell you because I wouldn't want to burden you with that knowledge.

I would rather kill myself than hurt you, and yet you think I don't think about you or take your situation into consideration. I have given you my soul, and you have given me pain.

So no, you are not the victim.

All I ever did was show you love, and all you ever did was take it.

Someone

July 18, 2024

Confronting the one you love can be devastating. I had been ignored time and time again by someone who claimed to love me. Yet in my time of need, she was absent. How can someone be so cold as to simply ignore the ones they care about? If I would have died, I wouldn't think she would regret not talking to me. Even if she was the only thing that could have helped.

When I was around you, I felt like there was hope. There was a reason to stay because I cared about someone, and they cared about me.

All this time wasted as I feel the truth: you don't love me anymore.

After I was hospitalized, you asked for space and time. Fuck me, did you even take a moment to think about how those demands would affect someone who's suicidal? After giving you space and writing to you, you just ignored me. Again, not helping my situation.

On July 16, I asked what we were. Two days later, you said we were not quite lovers, but very good friends with the possibility of getting together again.

I simply said that I cannot be in that. You're someone who avoids the person they proclaim to love. So if you're done with wanting space, come find me, and we can be together. But for now, we're nothing.

And that's when her teeth showed up.

She started accusing me of a lack of caring and thinking about her situation.
How the fuck can she be so ignorant to think this? I only thought of her, and she is one of the reasons I am in the hospital. I gave you all of me, but you keep taking, and taking more and more. And what am I left with? Not even a pulse. Now that you've broken me, you start to "say" I wasn't worthy. We never kissed, you never said the words "I love you" to me. How caring is that? I tried to kill myself, and you leave and attack me.
I want you to know that if I don't make it through this, my flowing blood will be your doing.
I hate that it ended this way. I hate that I still love you when you don't love me. I can't look at you without hearing the voices calling my name to the knives.
 I will no longer be a part of your life. I will no longer be welcome into the walls of your home, the comfort of your embrace, and the soft tone of your voice. And it fucking hurts.
 I never thought you would be the reason I would learn to hate myself.
 My love, you were blind to my sacrifice, and now I have to pay for that.

FIVE
CONTEMPLATING ALONE

The silence is so loud

Being occupied is a tactic I use. Having something to do is infinitely better than nothing.
 It may be a video game, developing friendships, or even writing. But when I am left alone
with nothing to do, the thoughts start to come out. They are all-consuming and destructive.
They cripple me down into a husk. Once I start to let in those thoughts, I break.
 The thoughts are scary when I feel this way. Living a life I don't want, breathing air I don't
deserve. The future is not bright; it's just a nightmare on the horizon. Every day, I get closer
to that nightmare. I realize I don't want to live, and it hurts like nothing else. The total
devastation hits one's soul.
 Sitting alone, not blinking, the silence is so fucking loud.
 The silence is a thousand screams of torture from hell itself. The silence is an invitation to
look into the void and accept the blissful option.

Numbness

The thoughts are dangerous. My body kicks into fight or flight and starts to play dead. I go
numb. I start to feel uncomfortable in the body I have. Textures feel off as the brain hammers
with a mighty headache. It keeps a hold on me throughout the whole day. I stop eating,
sleeping, and drinking. I am just in the moment, 24/7. The acceptance and embracing of the
pain and hurting that's flowing through that demonic vessel called your body.
You are defeated, you are broken. In this state, you don't even look for death; you are
beyond killing yourself, and you just break. You give in and let the void swallow you whole.
The thoughts are disturbing flashes of horrible scenarios you play on repeat in your head.
It fills my body, starting from the stomach. It spreads like a black hole, like a leak in the
system. It slowly takes over as I go numb, purposeless. Depression is a state of mind that
wants to stay in the darkness. Having to fight myself on such a scale, constantly denying my
body the satisfaction of emotion. It feels like hell, a constant punishment for what I know not

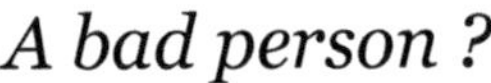

A bad person ?

When do you realize you are a bad person?

The scenarios I play in my head are so messed up, yet I keep playing them over and over until I fucking go insane.

I want to take a close friend out with me on a walk in the woods, just to turn to them, look them straight in the eye, and see their expression as I pull a knife out of my pocket and put it to my throat, against the soft and tender flesh. I would ask them to give me a reason to keep living. Little do they know, I've already made my choice. Therefore, I would get one last look at the reaction of a friend who cares, as I use the knife and the blood starts to spray out of my neck like a sprinkler.

I would picture a group of people shooting up my whole school while I wander through the main building, watching all my friends and everyone I care about getting brutally killed without mercy. Leaving me as the sole survivor.

If I hold a knife, I start to wonder what it would feel like to stab the person next to me with it.

I would stand up in the cafeteria and kill myself in a dramatic way.

The one I hate the most is the school shooting. I would like to clarify that I have no desire to hurt others. That, however, doesn't change the fact that these thoughts were in my brain and played over and over, like torture. Dripping insanity into my mind bit by bit.

I would raise the gun and start to shoot wildly, every shot taking another person someone loves. Each shot saves me a deeper place in hell. I would look my friends in the eyes as I pulled the trigger. The desperate look of betrayal and lack of understanding is so haunting. Hearing them scream out in pain and anger: "Welcome to my world." I let the silence come in and bring those screams of hell to the surface, death after death. I have become the grim reaper, listening to the people closest to me pleading for their lives while I look them in the eye, not giving any mercy. Seeing them bleed out, staining the floor, soaking my shoes in crimson red blood. I would walk coldly by those I deem unworthy of my time as I hunted down the last of my friends, witnessing their final moments. Each kill is not made with pleasure, but it's a form of self-harm by harming others.

Thinking about me standing in those halls with a stack of corpses, I would make myself the final victim of the massacre, knowing that if I leave, they would leave too. They don't deserve

to die. So why do I keep thinking these thoughts? Am I a bad person? Am I a fucking monster?

Is it your personality? You like it, don't you? The pain is a comfort for you. It's all you are. You're addicted to it. You can't leave it, you're not strong enough to leave it behind.

What can you do if you are lost in yourself, in your own emotion? Society can't help you, no one can help you anymore. You are all alone, like a fly trapped in a spider's web. You are helplessly waiting for the suffering to end.

It's taking over slowly, leaving nothing and taking everything bit by bit until there is nothing of the old you left. Until you are unrecognizable to the person you were before.

At first, it will take your energy, then your feelings, friends, later your sanity, and finally, once it is satisfied with your suffering, it will take your life.

In the end, you're no longer human. In the end, you're nothing but bones trapped, suffocating around flesh. At one point, you will look at your reflection and see nothing but a monster. Your personality has been sacrificed for your survival. You cast your friends aside as you try to hold onto life. You are truly a bad person, aren't you?

You should do everyone a favor and just end it all right here, right now.

Contemplating alone

"This isn't over, and the scars I have gotten are permanent. I will never forget that night when I held the knife to my throat. I will not forget her and how she saved me from taking that overdose that one time at school. I can't hold a knife the same way anymore. I can't forget all the times I was so close. Every time I feel joy in my life, I keep thinking about how I would have missed that feeling and that moment if I had ended it back then.

I won't forget the time I prayed out, saying, 'Mom, Dad, I just can't do it anymore.'

That sentence, that music, still fucks me up every time I hear it.

I am far from fixed. I am still sad, but it's getting better, and that's good.

I am scared I will be sad like this for a very, very long time, and I am scared of what will happen when I leave my support by the end of the year, just two weeks from now. I am scared of everything, but I am willing to look to the future for the first time in a long time. I see pain in the future. I see darkness in the future, but I finally see a future, and I don't want to feel like this anymore. Not again. Never again."

The paragraph above was written as a diary entry one week before I attempted to end my life.

It's funny how hope can backstab someone so violently.

Thinking... I am so tired of thinking, of contemplating the same things over and over without doing something about it, without truly letting my demons out.

The rain hits the roof. I can hear it violently pouring down the tiles. I have held the thoughts off long enough.

The void swallows me once again. The bliss takes control. I let it in and opened my mind to the voices.

I coldly evaluate the pros and cons of the life I have, putting people I care about into little boxes. Now, they are just cold, hard numbers. That's what their love has boiled down to. Every time I come up short by a country mile. There are always more reasons to end it than there ever are to keep living in this hell. If you can't move forward, then why even have legs? The numbness hits me as the worrying starts to set in. My lack of caring about myself follows me everywhere I go, every single day.

It's not getting better; I'm just getting used to it.

I know it will all be so much easier if I killed myself, and my body doesn't try to object. It doesn't resist. I wouldn't say I want to die. Sure, if I could push a button and be happy again, I would. But that's not how life works, and I don't want to go through the pain of my existence anymore. I let the music consume me as I choose to exist in the moment of suffering. My eyes are still, and my brain is done. My heart beats faster, and my arms and legs shake uncontrollably.

It always leads to war. I just want to go to sleep. I am so, so... tired.

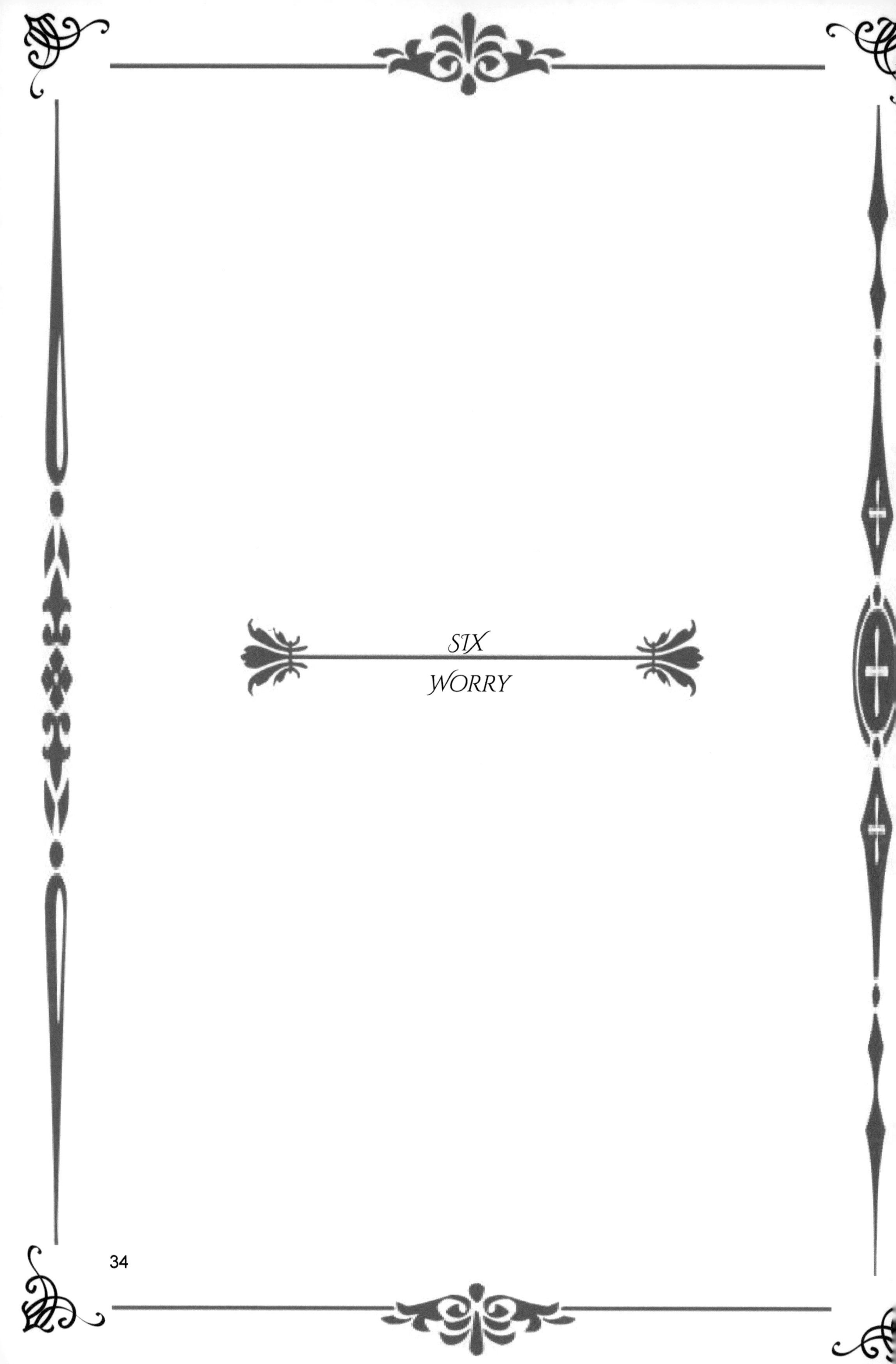

SIX
WORRY

Battle

It's a battle every single day. This disease inside of me is killing me slowly. It takes everyone and everything around me. It took my friends. It took my lover. It took my old self. It took away my ability to feel and love. It takes and takes, not caring when I break.

The fight to keep myself chained to this realm takes every bit of energy I have left. This war is endless. I can't keep bleeding.

I worry about the future. I don't want to see the future. The future probably has me in a better situation. I would be happy. I would have new friends and connections with people I care about. But I can't go through the amount of pain it takes to get there. I am not strong enough to see that life on the other side.

There is a way for it to get better, and if I keep looking, I will find it. But the numbness takes over. It drives me to extremes and danger. It keeps me up at night, calling me to end it. I can feel my grip slipping. And the scary thing is, there is nothing I can think of that I want anymore. I simply have no reason to wake up every day. So why even wake up?

I go through this every day. It's a constant pain that cannot be described. I am not alone in this pain, and others have it worse, but I don't care. I am fighting a battle, and knowing they are fighting doesn't change the fact that I am losing. I am losing.

Breaking a promise

I can feel it growing, the lack of caring is back. I made a promise, one of staying on this earth. It's a promise I might have to break soon. It's just not getting better, and every day where it's not getting better, it just gets worse. It's testing my patience. It's rising to my absolute limit.

I am scared of what I will do to myself. I can't stop it anymore. One of these days, it will happen. I can't feel my own heart anymore. My body and mind are so fucking silent; they're not responding to my thoughts and feelings. What is this feeling I have? I can't control it. I am not in control of my body. My emotions have hijacked my brain, and they are driving me into a wall.

What can I do to keep the promise I gave to those I care about? The world has given me a reason to live. That reason is to keep others happy. I can't find happiness in my own torture. I

am giving so much just by living right now, and I think people should realize this and respect the fact that I go through all this pain to keep a single promise.

But I am slipping, and starting to get irrational. That's scary. Yet I think it's time for me to think for myself for once and break a promise. I don't want to hurt anyone anymore, but the simple fact of living is just too painful to bear.

Your worst enemy

My worst enemy is myself. I am my own reason for dying. I can't change this. I fight my mind every day, losing my sanity bit by bit. I don't think much is left now. I can't take this much longer. I must silence the voices, the thoughts, the demons. The bottom is close.

I am scared and afraid of myself. I am going to be the reason I kill myself. The mind is so fucking scary sometimes. I am starting to get comfortable with the thought of dying, of the last small price of pain I have to give to end it. The feeling of a knife jammed into my throat is starting to calm me; it's peace to think of my blood flowing out of me. What have I become? The human in me is lost and gone.

I need to get over the last hurdles before I can convince my mind that I am ready to leave. My mind is rushing things. I have my options available for ending it. They aren't pretty, but they would work. It will work.

Soon, it will all be over.

Worry

I worry about disappointing my mom and dad. I'm ready to die, but they're not ready to accept it. I'm scared of what it will do to them; they're a roadblock that makes this all feel so fucking hard. How can I hurt them like this? I don't want to hurt them. Hurting people seems to be the only thing I'm good at anymore. I bring sadness and worry to everyone who gets too close to me. I wish my friends would forget about me, so I could make their pain easier. But instead, I drag them down my spiral.

How many times can I ask for help, knowing they can't provide it?
 I've given and given, and all I ask for is something in return. Yet, I don't feel fulfilled. My life feels unfulfilled; I still have wants and needs. I want to be close to someone who actually cares. I want to feel worthy, not break every day. I want to be proud of something instead of feeling angry at nothing. I want to live my life to the fullest, not at the end of a knife.

I worry. I can't stop myself from doing something that will hurt people or end my chance at happiness. I'm not ready to go, but I can't stop myself. I worry about the future because I don't see myself in it. All I see is the sadness that will come from my absence, but I can't resist the pull of the bliss.

What must I do to escape this mess without hurting them? I care too much to hurt them with a wound so deep. I don't think my parents would ever recover from it. It feels like it would lead to more death, more chaos. Knowing that I might be the cause of their suffering feels like a curse. I'm punished if I live, and punished if I die.

I choose to hurt myself instead of them, but I can't keep it up. I'm breaking. I can only take so many punches. Death isn't the easy option like people say. It's the option of those who've fought, again and again, constantly getting back up when they're knocked down. Suicide is the option of the warrior who, after countless attempts, finally fails to get back up. And so, they declare defeat. Tell me— is that warrior a coward, or someone who was matched by a stronger force?

I worry because I'm no longer scared. I'm no longer in the mindset of living. I worry because I'm ready to surrender. I can't get back up anymore, so all I can do is sit around and wait for something to happen. And I know what's most likely to happen. That's why I'm scared. That's why I worry.

SEVEN
GUARDIAN ANGEL

Guardian angel

I hate my life; I can't keep this up. The pills were supposed to help, but they don't help enough.

I thought it was over, but no, it's still here and it's still building pressure. I don't know how to find the strength to keep fighting it. I am scared because I just lost my hope. I have nowhere left to go, and I don't want to try again anymore. I just can't seem to get rid of this feeling. My body is tired out; I won't last forever like this.

I didn't ask to be born, I didn't ask for my life to be like this. I don't like this anymore. My life is filled with hate and pain at everything. I am breaking, and I can't seem to find a way to get some peace.

I have tried again and again to be the best possible person I could, helping where it's needed, setting others before myself, caring, and showing that I am there for someone. And what am I left with? Me wanting to kill myself 1,000 times over. It hurts so much; I don't deserve this treatment. I have tried so hard to be there, and I am paid back in blood, pain, and torment. It's so unjust. There are many who are more deserving of this feeling. Why can't I get what I want? I try and try and try to be there for others, and they are never there for me. Even if I treat them better than good, it ends the same. Somehow, I am not enough. For them, it's never enough.

I don't like myself anymore; my core is shattered. All that's left of someone trying to pick himself up is destroying everything around him. I don't want to see myself destroyed anymore, so I will kill the monster inside of me, the only way I know how.

I have been beaten, I am broken and bleeding, and I am losing more blood than they can give me. My destiny is set. I don't want to feel the foul hope again. It hurts so much.

Why doesn't she love me the same way I love her? Am I not deserving of that? What's wrong with me? I am trying to be there, but it seems I only fuck it up. I don't know how to help, but I am trying. But this help goes deeply unappreciated. I have given so much, and they just keep taking and taking. I am in pain, so fucking help me! Are you blind, or do you just not care? Do you hate me, for fuck's sake?

I have lost the fire inside me. I can't see past the fog in my head, and I am done with caring about my own well-being. I want to let go so badly. I want to give in and just do it. Nothing but rage is left. I am about to explode with emotion, and I am ready for this time to be the last.

They didn't care.

They didn't listen.

They didn't help.

They just took more.

It didn't end the way it should have.

I am not happy anymore. I am not living anymore. I am alone. My soul is gone, and I can't... I just fucking can't.

Mom and Dad, I am sorry I won't be coming home this time. I won't be sleeping in the same bed anymore. I love you, and I can't see you both fade because of my absence. You tried everything in your power to help me, and it did help. This is not you failing as parents. I am just not a human anymore. I just can't keep on living this way. I can't keep looking forever. I can't keep being here, for this is not a life that's worth living.

The truth:

The truth is, I don't want to leave. I don't want to kill myself. I am desperate, looking around, trying to find something to hold onto. I ask for a reason and get nothing. I don't have a reason to wake up or do anything. I have no one I want to see and nothing I want to do. I don't want food or drinks. I don't want to cry or be sad. I just don't want to do anything anymore. I just want it to end. I want it all to just end. Why, oh fucking God, why didn't it end that day at the school? I would have died happier than I will be now.

I am past the point of no return. I am breaking the promise. I can't feel it in my body. It's lurking. I need something to save me now, not later, but now. I need fucking help because I am sinking, drowning. My grip is slipping, and no one is there to save me. I need a solution. I don't know what it can be, but I need something, fucking something to save me. I can't go. Help. I don't see a future anymore. I don't expect to see the future anymore. I just see death. I can feel it calling me so fucking bad. I can't resist it anymore. I need something to help me get out of this body. I need my guardian angel to show its face and give me justice. I don't deserve this, do I? Do I?

Am I a bad person? Am I getting something twisted? Am I blinded by my own beliefs to the point that I don't see the evil within? I see my flaws, but maybe I don't see the scope of the flaws. I am draining the goodwill of everyone around me. Am I a disease that takes and takes? Am I manifesting the sickness within, spreading it outwards? It seems I don't have a guardian angel. But is it because I am not worthy, or is it because I am the disease? Will I find redemption in death? I can at least find peace in it.

40

This angel is too late. I search for a cure but find nothing. Why must I turn into a number, one of the many that have suffered the same fate as me? Humans with a soul simply reduced to a mere number, a statistic to show how the disease is spreading. I am simply another soul in the spiral, and my time is nearing its end. The spiral cuts through the earth all the way down to hell. I am losing hope and don't see a way out. Life has just gotten worse from trying. I am sick to the core of feeling anything at all. Fake feeling, real feeling, I don't care anymore. I just don't care. The heavens have abandoned me, and no one is coming to save me. I am alone and ready to take the next step into the blissful void.

EIGHTH
THE BOTTOM OF THE SPIRAL

I have decided

26 July 2024, 12:21:

As I write this, I have made my choice, and in these last days, I have gathered my strength to end it all. I have a few locations in mind, each one carefully chosen—it feels like an art project. This is me trying to express it to whoever cares to listen.

Here it is: the bottom of the spire.

I cannot go lower; it cannot hurt anymore. I am broken beyond repair. I no longer see the point in keeping up the fight, and I am more than ready to go. I have a knife with me and have tested it, it can work. I don't feel it anymore. I can't feel anything; it has been so long since I was happy. I just can't keep living like this. I have, at this point, made my decision. I am... I... I am not getting through this.

Consequences

There are always consequences. I have broken my family; my mom and dad are used up, their love shining, but their capacity is filled. I am ready to die, but I can't do it because of them, because of the consequences. I hear the demons calling me, and I've hit a point of contempt where I no longer want to live. I have made my decision. But the realization that this is serious hits me. I am now going to break the promise I gave. I am going to let them down. I am giving into my dark, twisted desire to end it.

But when I see the worried faces of my parents, I break again. Those faces haunt me. I saw them after my failed attempt.

If I keep this up, I will continue to break. I will take drugs and alcohol. I will hurt myself, taking no pleasure in the person I have become, looking back at the things I've done. I have made many mistakes. What's one more going to do? I don't want to leave this world behind. I can't forfeit my chance to be a bigger part of others' lives. There are so, so many consequences. I can silence them all with one simple trick. It's only…

The bottom of the spiral

Rage fills my body as anger and frustration overwhelm what little humanity is left in my bones. I can no longer muster the strength to deny myself. I am not living my life, and there is nothing I want. There is nothing anyone can do anymore. It's too late for me. To all who knew me, I'm sorry to have disappointed you. My existence has been a blessing for many people, but for me, it has been a curse — one given by the gods. The universe is so cruel. I fight for my justice and get nothing back. I'm just left with anger, an empty anger without guidance.

The silence of my body screams surrender. My brain no longer pushes dark thoughts away. I just accept them. I am so tired. I just want to sleep. I didn't get peace. I didn't get the justice I was looking for. I am left beaten. I don't know who can help me. I just want to be held by someone. I just want the warm embrace of a loving soul to comfort me. I just want safety, because I am not safe. I haven't been safe for a long time. I can't run from myself. I can't fight myself. I can't stop waking up just to be reminded of why I have these scars.

I am not ready to leave this world. I want to see so much more of it. I want to experience the friendships I could have, the children I might one day have. I long for normality. I just want to have a normal fucking life. I'm only fucking 18. That's too young to fucking go. There is so much I want. Is it too much to ask for something I want but cannot get? Now it's too late. I can't stop myself, and I don't really want others to stop me because I can't take another minute of this pain, of this purgatory, out of place and time. It's so dark down here. I don't want to be in the dark.

Hello, help me, anyone. I can't see anymore. I am blinded. It's so dark in the void. It's so dark. It's so lonely. Where is the exit? I can't find the way out. I am down here with so many lost souls, but I feel alone. How can I be surrounded by loving people yet feel so alone? I need comfort. I need light. I need something. I am scared. I am scared. I am fucking scared. Help me out. I need to get out. It's so dark. It's so dark. I never knew it could get this dark, this cold. I will take the only way out of the dark I know of — the only way.

He falls to the ground, crying and screaming out into the void, screaming for help. Nobody came to his aid. No one saved him.

The ever-growing void took him deeper, getting closer, but he could go no further. He was left to rot by the sideline. He felt alone and trapped. The demons had corrupted his soul, and there was nothing left. There was only one thing he could do to escape the dread of that void. Each day he didn't choose those options, the void just took him deeper. Deeper and deeper down the spiral.

# NINE
SEE THE SUN GO DOWN

Standing in the backyard, looking out at the sky, it's so peaceful, it's near blissful.
It's so quiet in nature. Nature does not care about anything. The sun lights the clouds in an orange aura. The day has been so beautiful, so peaceful. The sky is painted in strokes of red and orange, like a beautiful canvas. The sun paints its larger-than-life glory.
There are only a few birds out by now. They are chirping and singing, their tone just right for the ear. Standing on the wooden boards, looking out to the field of golden corn ready for harvest. Your feet are firmly placed, almost sinking into the old boards which nature has overgrown with grass and leaves. A calm, chilling breeze rolls in and kisses your exposed lips, gently greeting the neck and mixing with the warmth from your body, generated by your blood pumping valiantly through your veins.
The world can be such a charming place at times. All you need is nature and some peace of mind. My mind is at peace. Why? Isn't it clear to see?

It has finally made its mind up. It's finally quiet; it's taking it all in. It's the calm before the storm. It's the tide pulling itself to sea before the flood hits. It's the little peace you have left. It's the inevitable feeling that something is going to happen that is out of your control, and so you just don't fight it.
It's going to be today. I am feeling an emotional charge that will overwhelm me. The wave is on the horizon, and I am holding a knife. I begin walking to the chosen location. It's a beautiful forest bed with moss and birds. It's well secluded. It's peaceful and blissful. Like this sundowning. There is peace in the violence. When I don't see purpose in my life, I will simply connect to nature. Nature doesn't ask anything of you. Nature doesn't expect anything of you. Nature has already accepted you.
The wave of emotions can wait that little bit longer so I can just sit here and look at the sun. I can feel that this wave will be devastating, and my brain will go through all of the emotions. This time, I won't let them go. This time, I will fight them with a knife to the throat. I close my eyes and breathe in. The air fills my whole body. For once, I feel at home in it. For once, I feel happiness knowing that the end is near. I am finally committing and not backing down. I am afraid, but I am determined to go through with it.

My mind slowly wonders what could have been — to the life I could have had if I didn't do it. I could see a beautiful and loving wife. I would have children of my own and a job I was happy with. Life had its ups and downs, but the people around me would have made it worth experiencing. My mom and dad were still here and in good health. My sister would have become a fashion expert and an architect. That life sounds nice, but it's too far away for me

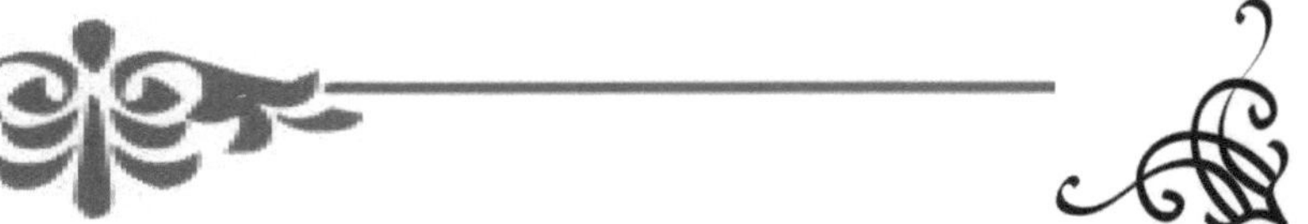

to reach it. Anger slowly fills. The feelings start to appear. I guess that was my final moment of peace.

This is it. This is the moment I die. My last days have been lived, and I will go to a new place now. I start walking to the location as the mind starts to weaponize itself. I grip the kitchen knife a little harder. Scars on my legs from battles lost with this knife are all over. Some new, some old. The wave is approaching, and I will choose bliss. In death, there is peace. So, I shall go find my deserving peace. There is no justice left in my world. There is only the sun going down, and my demons coming out.

The wave starts to break through, and I feel myself start to panic and worry. This is the last battle. Will I win it? And what does winning even mean for me? What is winning if it's just prolonging pain? Life isn't fair, and people can be cold, but this is my fate. Don't let it be yours.

TEN
THE ROAD TO BLISS

Convincing yourself

Every day it takes a different shape. It takes a part of my soul and it has turned me into someone else. Someone I don't recognize, my reflection is not my own anymore. The boy I was, I am no longer. The scars, the pain, slowly killing me a thousand times over. Each day adding more to my burden, It's not letting me go.

It's a never-ending marathon at full speed, it's not a question of if, but a question of when you choose to give in. *Not knowing when you will break*, not wanting everyone and everything around you to lose you.

I often feel like screaming, punishing and crying my heart out.
I feel like descending down a spiral of regret and suffering just to justify seeing the blissful end.
I can be happy, yet can be suicidal, *What am I?*

Most of the time death is an easier path. Death is a luxury my consciousness can't afford.

I try to avoid the sad *gaping void* calling me, *Bliss.*

I try to drown out the voices telling me to jump, to stand in front of the incoming car, to take the knife. Drowning it all with alcohol wasting the so-called life I have. My brain keeps over dramatising everything that's ever happened to me, again trying to justify taking the step into……. *bliss.*

"Death is a luxury my consciousness cant afford"

Thoughts from hell, whispers from heaven

The voices keep telling me how to be violent, always showing me the worst case scenario. If I take a knife and put it in my hand I think of cutting myself, going to bliss, and to murder someone, just to feel something. To set my path on a permanent fuck up.
I walk along a road, the voices tell me to *jump* in front of the oncoming car.
I stand near a cliff, they tell me to jump,
I look out a window, they say I should smash it with my head.

I stand alone somewhere at night, they tell me to run away and disappear.

I think of scenarios that truly horrifies me.
School shootings, *slitting my throat* in front of the whole school, looking at someone mass-murdering all my friends in front of me, and I doing nothing but watch, looking as everything I love burns. walking with someone into the woods, at a peaceful grove, one with birds and moss, I would look deeply into their eyes and slit my throat, to see their reaction, and to enter bliss with a smile on my lips. Calling my friends, telling them I am going to kill myself, and lessening to them, trying to justify my existence, hearing what i actually mean to them.
I dream of something bad happening to me so I can justify how I feel, *how this feels*, and what *I want to do.*

"We all think like monsters, but i find comfort in the darkness"

losing my humanity

I don't really feel happy anymore, I can't *trust* my own feelings anymore, *I can't trust myself anymore.*
who I was before is *dead* a thousand times over.
Each scar from each day, offering a little more of the *old me*, until nothing is left but an empty skeleton surrounded by flesh.
I am but a vessel , one that survived for so *long* it forgot what it was like to live.

The thoughts and lack of feelings, *makes me an animal*, I have forgotten to live, I only focused on surviving.
In the act of surviving you are only an animal, I am only an animal.
I have lost my *humanity*. I have lost my way, my meaning. My strife to be.
If I am not *human* in the mind but only the body and bones, then there is no reason to live amongst the *feral tribe* called *sociely*.
Give me purpose or give me *bliss*.

Don't just leave me with nothing.

"On only focusing on surviving, I became an animal"

Holding it together

Everyday, every minute, I try to keep it together, I try to not *break*.
To not give in to the fake feelings of despair.
It takes all your emotions and energy to deny your own feelings, not to push through them but to
downright deny them. It's going against the brain. It's a battle *you will lose* eventually.
Yet I smile and *act happy*, to try and mimic my friends, I so rarely get to show the *real me*.
I hold it all together *for them*, so they don't see the endless suffering I bring on myself every single
waking moment. I give a fake smile, I laugh and joke.   I always were good at acting.

At one point I will break, and *bring down hell* on everyone around me.
Losing all my *friends* and throwing myself out the edge.
The feeling of wanting to *punch someone*, to break with anger, to point the *blame* for all this pain.
To be angry at *someone else* then myself.
But for now I am holding it together knowing that *it won't last*, knowing that in the end
it's pointless to *keep fighting* battles when you know the war is lost.

"It's pointless to keep fighting the battle, when you know the war is lost"

Give me a light in the night

The voices are taking again,   *and I chose to listen.*
The knife called my name.   I answer,   the grip of the handle, is so familiar by now.

I can feel it calling, the calling of the *bliss.*
The hopelessness clouds my judgment, and I feel the danger of where I am heading.

I *need a friend* to come through the door,   *they never do.*
When I call them, they answer,   *yet they are never what I need.*

I need someone to guide me, to show me the path. *The path I need* to take to lend me the strength to
keep the *fight* alive.

I need someone to give me a light, because I am *stuck in the dark*, and my eyes are beginning to get
used to the dark. *getting used to hell.*

But this darkness is not a place to build a home, this isn't a place to plant your roots as *it will break you*, thinking you're out of the woods, not knowing you're more lost than you ever were.

Give me a light so I can find the path, or give me the light so I can burn the forest around me, *destroying everything within.*

I know I am not *alone, but I feel lonely.*

I know there's a way out of the darkness but *I don't know how long I can look* for it before I fade. I can't find it *on my own, I can't do this on my own. I am not strong enough* to battle with the *demons* that come out at night so *someone* give me a light.
I need someone to guide me, to find me, to help me when I *can't help myself.*

Yet all the help I have gotten hasn't given a light, it gives a glimpse of the other side, of the peace of mind and happiness there was before the woods.
It's torturing glimpses of what I could have if I fight, if I find that path, it's a *mirage of hope* in a hopeless wasteland of everyday *suffering, pain and rage.*
It's a faded memory of a *feeling that ceases to exist* in the darkness of the night.
When you have tried to find the path **yet fail** to find it, *where do you go from there?*

You go forward, you *go deeper* into the woods,
you realise there was always **one** *path* out of the woods, *bliss.*
you *choose it* when you have *looked without luck* for long enough.

I have looked long enough.
So I beg. Someone or something, show me the path to *eternal salvation*, and give me a second chance at a happy ending, at a *fulfilled life.* Give me something, for *I am lost*

"I have been in the darkness so long my eyes are adjusting to the pain"

Blame

With *pain* comes blame. With all the **emotion** *filling up*, *you seek someone* to point to.

As I look for that person *I don't find anything* but a room filled with mirrors.
 Every time I find *someone* I want to say is *to blame* for my pain, I point at them and *they are* *replaced* by a mirror.
The rage I feel *overfiles* my body and *makes me angry* at every small thing someone might *fuck up* around me, meaning I have *unreasonable behaviour* with anger at random small things.

And *my rage comes out* on those *not deserving*, on that part I can only blame myself.
With each telling of an emotion, I lose a part of myself to my **inner desire** of *wanting to feel sad*.
There the blame is only pointed towards myself.
To those who have *wronged* me I simply don't get angry with them as most *were* friends.
On that I can only blame *myself*.
Everyone I point the *blame* to gets replaced with a mirror, leaving only my reflection pointing to the only one that's too blame, *myself.* **I am the reason for the fake feelings**
 I over dramatise,
I *am to blame* for the words **I** choose to tell *others*,
I am to blame for **not** *getting better*,   for **not** *waking up*, for **not** stopping and fighting,
and realising that I am okay but it's my *brain* that thinks I am not.
The blame falls on ME.   **I AM TO BLAME!!!!**

Therefore I hate myself, **for being** my worst enemy.

The rage is pointed towards myself, therefore I must punish myself.
I slowly close my eyes with tears as the *knife starts to call* my name again.

"Everytime I point my finger to blame someone, I only see my reflection pointing back"

Overflow

I can't live in my body with the extreme rage, frustration and sadness possessing me.
My heartbeat speeds up, I can hear it ringing in my ears, as a *headache starts* to sharply pierce my
forehead, like a *drill* drilling through the back of my skull, my hands *shake* and *veins* start to
appear as my breathing gets short and snappy.
My brain *can't think straight anymore* as it tries to suppress the primal instinct
of exploding in rage and breaking the walls, doors and windows.
Sounds around me become *deadly fires*, and   I am the fuse.
Actively looking for the fire, waiting for that one thing that will *tip the scale.*

It becomes hard to focus on seeing and to communicate normally.
The stomach is like a *hurricane.* My head is like a storm in the sea, with waves of *panic* on a
small fishing boat way out of its depth. The **sounds** peers meaning and I close my fist ready
to burst into an animal. Now no one can help. Now I show my **teeth.**
Ready to attack. Barely able to breath, the little humanity and reason of my soul is locked in the
trunk, and the blind emotion and desire has the keys to the car. I have lost the ability to choose

"Society try as they must, can't change a man which emotion has taken over"

Screaming in the silence

An empty *vessel* walking next to *friends*, no one can hear its screams for help. *No one* is taking
it seriously. "Do they think it's too scared to *do it* ?". Is it a test ?, *What must it prove*
to get them to wake up and realise it's not okay, **that it's far from okay, it's barely hanging on**
and has said so to the so-called friends.
What must **it do**, hurt itself, **kill itself** ? Just to prove a point. *Crying* itself to sleep every
night, wishing it never existed in the first place.
Crying for help knowing no one will EVER be **enough** to keep **It** in this realm.

It looks for salvation in the dark, as it tries to find the help in the light,
yet the light does nothing,
it has given up and hopelessly builds emotion ready to **break,**

ready to accept the *darker path*.

The ***emotional monster*** is *too much* as the tears run down its face,
as the monster comes out and it looks up and it sees nothing but itself, left by society, left by friends, left by the side of **everything**.

It cracks and breaks as the **emotion** *takes over* and its humanity shines through as the **weight** of **everything** comes down. *It dies,* slowly bleeding out with silent screams meant for a guardian angel yet its meet with nothing but its **demons**

"Silent screams are meant for the angels but are answered by your demons"

Break

Screaming loudly, **not caring about who hears it**, I can hardly breathe because the **emotion** is **choking me**,

as I **break** into a thousand different pieces. **I run down the road** *screaming* up at the universe, why me, **what have I done to deserve this**, no one should feels this way, **have I not suffered enough**, give me something please **god give me salvation** give me peace **give me something I** DON'T want to die, **I don't want the** *bliss*, I cant **kill myself**, not now, not hear.
I can't go, **I won't go, I have a family** waiting for me to come **home**. I want to go home, I don't know where **home** is anymore but **I want it**. I cant keep **doing this, I can't handle it anymore, somebody FUCKING HELP ME PLEASE**... **please** I need help. **I can't** do this on my own. **I am not strong enough** and I am too close to the edge. I can't **fail** my friends, my family, myself.
Don't let me do this to myself, don't **make** me ***end*** it please **I beg you**.
Screaming up at the sky as its the last thing I can do, **alone, left, BETRAYED, FUCKED by the things that would have helped,** cursed by myself. RAGE FRUSTRATION AND DESPAIR feels every part of my body as I am **blinded** by sadness and adrenalin for the utter mix of a melting man I have become. **Punching the walls, breaking** the stones, **ripping** out my own hair, tearing the flesh from my arms. *Giving in too the emotion* letting the animal come out broken, **none human, ripping screams** of **anguish** and **desperate** cries for **help**. Knowing the battle is lost. Tears run down soaking the beard, glazing the desperate look in my eyes. As I scream.

So hurt me again! I have LOST! I am BROKEN! I am *BEATEN!* BEYOND REPAIR!.
So twist the fucking! knife! and hurt me some more because I want to feel it!, It's the only thing I know anymore. **Pain, suffering,   IT'S OVER YOU WIN YOU DID IT   I AM DONE   I'M DONE WITH EVERYTHING, THE BATTLE IS WON   THE LAST LINE OF DEFENCE IS BROKEN   I AM BROKEN**.... **I**... I am Brocken. The words leave my mouth as a soft and sober tone fills my head and a feeling of acceptance fills me.

"To live in hell is bad, but to feel like your not living is worse"

There's fear in letting go

A heavenly slow piano-like sound feels my body as it accepts its fate. I have accepted that I am going to leave this world and no longer be part of it. Goodbye friends, lover and family. I wont see my friends grow up or be a bigger **part of their lives.** I have forfeited my own chance at something more. **I truly can't say** sorry **enough times for what I am going to do,** the truth is I know that somewhere, Somehow there is a way out, **that somewhere that is a happy ending,** and I know that I am not going to find that ending, **I don't want** death **but I just can't live anymore.** Mom.. Dad .. I **am scared, I really don't want to go.** I really don't want to **take the step** into the **bliss**. I want to be held by you, **I didn't want any of this.** hold me a little bit, could you not?. Im scared I am so **fucking** sceared, **I dont want to go, hold me a little, couse if I go,** I want to go surrounded by those I love the most. **Mom, dad help me pls**, I can't stop myself. **I want a way out please, you have always been able to help me, so help me somehow. I don't wanna go,** I don't wanna go **please. I can't leave you, I can't. Please help me, just help me,** I can't do this anymore. I can't, **i won't**, mom dad if you care don't let me go, please don't let me go, I don't wanna go. I am so so scared. **I want my old me back.** I just want to be **happy**, I just want to be *fucking* **happy**, is that really **to much** to **ask for.** hold me while I fade **I just wish that you could hold me forever**, I am not ready to die, I am not ready to say goodbye...
Mom.. dad... **know that I love you and there was nothing you could have done to change this,** you have been the best part of **my life** and you where more than ***someone like me could ever have asked for***,
I am sorry for what I am going to do,   please.... forgive me,

I know your lives are hard enough as it is, and I am so sorry I **wont be there** to make it easier in your **darkness**.

I love you with the last part of my soul and you know perhaps in the next life we will meet again. **You** have not failed as parents, I have failed as a son... mom.... dad... I LOVE YOU..Goodbye and thank you for being who you are.

"You didn't fail as parents, I failed you as a son"

The calling of the bliss

The mind is set,   the knife is sharp,   tears softly lick my chin as my legs shake.

So this is how it ends.

Alone with myself listening to the birds,
 peacefulness filled the air as every moment felt like a million.
I touched the grass looking out on the forest holding the kitchen knife, looking at it.
The mind is at peace knowing you have made a choice.
Peaceful sounds and a quiet nothingness rings in the air.
For once in as long as you can remember, you feel happy and calm, there's nothing to stress about.
Nothing more to think about. Nothing more to bleed pointlessly for.
My thoughts go through letting go of everything and everyone. Goodbye my love, goodbye my friends, goodbye family.
All the things that were the good things in my life.
All the small things. A feeling of almost HAPPINESS fills me as a smile breaks upon my lips.
Every moment feels good when you know your time is limited,
and my final moments are ones of happiness and peace of mind,
the ring of an almost heavenly slow violin, taking its time, a sound of acceptance.
 this is how it ends, this is where it ends, my final words have been spoken and soon my final thoughts will have been through.

 I raise the knife up to meet my throat. as a tear rolls down my cheek I close my eyes. The last thing I see is a beautiful forest bed of moss grass and blue skies. It's so blissful, nature.

I think of my love and my mom and dad, picturering them all. Don't worry, I won't ever forget you or leave you because the last thing I did was see you, the last light that fades, my breath slows down, as I feel the bliss approaching..
The knife cuts as the smile gets bigger.

A lifeless body falls on the moss hitting the ground with blood streaming out. The birds still sing, the world still turns, blissfully unaware. Another life lost to its emotion. Another soul betrayed by society, another soul abandoned. Just another soul answering …. Answering the call to the

BliSs...

"Rest now in the comfort of your choice, rest now in the void"

Bliss

Bliss is the comfort of simply not believing in the afterlife. It's the understanding that once you end your life, you lose all recognition of time, how you were, and how you are. You just float around in eternal contempt, like a fish happy with its simple existence. In bliss, you don't need meaning or purpose. You don't waste time because time no longer exists. It's a place where you neither live nor feel sadness, and therefore, you are forever happy. It sounds like heaven to me.

But this bliss is not worth it. I have attempted suicide twice with pills and have self-harmed. There is always another path to try—please keep this in mind because the fight is worth it. Most days, I don't feel hope for the future, but I know I will see it. You are not alone in your fight. Whether someone gave this to you or you bought it yourself, you are reading this because you are trying to help yourself. With time, things will get better. I promise you that.

Thank you for supporting me. This is my first novel and my first work as a writer, and I'm struggling with many diagnoses and mental illnesses. Your support helps me on my journey to get better, and I hope my writing can help or enlighten you, even just a little bit.

© 2024 Mark Gould

Publisher: BoD · Books on Demand, Strandvejen 100,

2900 Hellerup, bod@bod.dk

Print: Libri Plureos GmbH, Friedensallee 273,

22763 Hamborg, Tyskland

ISBN: 978-87-7691-553-7